IMAGES
of Sport

HIBERNIAN
FOOTBALL CLUB
1875-1975

Gordon Smith – one of football's great masters.

IMAGES
of Sport

HIBERNIAN

FOOTBALL CLUB

1875-1975

Compiled by
Paul Lunney

TEMPUS

First published 2001
Copyright © Paul Lunney, 2001

Tempus Publishing Limited
The Mill, Brimscombe Port,
Stroud, Gloucestershire, GL5 2QG

ISBN 0 7524 2170 0

Typesetting and origination by
Tempus Publishing Limited
Printed in Great Britain by
Midway Clark Printing, Wiltshire

Centre forward Alan Gordon is tackled by Rangers defender Tom Forsyth at Ibrox in 1972.

Contents

Hibernian postcard from around 1900.

Introduction

Hibernian Football Club was founded in 1875 at a meeting of St Patrick's Catholic Young Mens' Society in St Mary's Street Halls, Edinburgh. Co-founders were Father Hannan and Michael Whelahan; the latter became the team's first captain and proposed the club's name, Hibernia being Latin for Ireland.

The early years of the new club were fraught with difficulties. Their application for membership of the SFA and EFA was rejected on the grounds that Hibernian were 'Irish' not Scottish, but with perseverance and support from leading local teams Hibs eventually gained entrance to both football organizations. Slowly but surely Edinburgh's Green Jerseys progressed, and with three consecutive Scottish Cup semi-final appearances in 1884, 1885 and 1886 they knew their day would come sooner rather than later. So it proved.

In 1887 Hibernian became the first club to take the Scottish Cup out of the West of Scotland, and they topped that fantastic feat at the beginning of the following season by beating the not-so-'invincible' Preston North End 2-1 for the title 'Champions of the World'.

The Hibs side of 1887 glittered like a galaxy with names that would live forever – like that of the dribbling genius Willie Groves and the brilliant half-back line of McGhee, McGinn and McLaren.

Celtic Football and Athletic Club formed in November 1887 and after Hibernian inaugurated their stadium on 8 May 1888 in a friendly against Cowlairs, the fledgling club from the East End of Glasgow decided it wished to be the game's giant. The club proceeded to entice Hibs' best players to Parkhead, an underhanded action which resulted in Gallagher, McKeown, McLaren and Groves all defecting to the West. This turn of events was a severe blow to Hibernian and in 1891 the club went defunct.

Seasons 1891/92 and 1892/93 therefore consisted mainly of Hibs putting their affairs in order and trying to find a new ground. Thankfully, by February 1893 both objectives had been met, with re-admittance to the SFA and the East of Scotland FA and a new Easter Road stadium. The resurrected Hibernian soon found their feet and quickly triumphed in the Edinburgh Cup, the Roseberry Charity Cup and the Second Division Championship in both the 1893/94 and 1894/95 seasons.

A 'Blue Riband' final defeat by arch-rivals Hearts at Logie Green in 1896 meant the Green Jerseys had to bide their time in their quest for glory, although close to the peak of Scottish football in the late 1890s. At the turn of the century they would reach the mountain top, with Scottish Cup glory in 1902 against Celtic and the League Championship title in 1903. The talented team at that time included the superb shot-stopper Harry Rennie, brilliant half-back Barney Breslin, the devastating attacker Johnny Divers, cute playmaker Paddy Callaghan and the unforgettable skipper and Welsh winger Bobby Atherton.

The club reached the 'Blue Riband' final again in 1914, but lost 4-1 to Celtic after a replay. Under the managership of Alec Maley, Hibernian subsequently played in Scottish Cup finals back-to-back in 1923 and 1924, only to finish runners-up on both occasions. The Hibees fielded many wonderful footballers in the early 1920s, such as goalkeeping great Bill Harper, goal poacher Jimmy McColl and little 'Wembley Wizard', 'Ginger' Dunn.

From 1925 until the outbreak of the war in 1939, the Capital Greens struggled to survive in the top flight; indeed, they were relegated in 1931 and starred in the lower league for two terms.

In 1936, Willie McCartney was put in charge and brought back some much-needed prestige to Easter Road. Unforunately, big 'Mac' died on 24 January 1948 just as the team he reared was about to take the League flag. Hugh Shaw took over McCartney's mantle and with the advent of the fabulous 'Famous Five' forward-line of Smith, Johnstone, Reilly, Turnbull and Ormond, Hibernian became the finest side in the country with Championship success in 1951 and 1952. In 1955/56 Hibernian were the sole representatives of Great Britain in the inaugural European Cup competition and reached the penultimate stage before losing to French club Rhiems.

The 1960s saw some European glory nights at Easter Road with marvellous victories over Real Madrid and Napoli. However, with the constant selling of star performers such as Willie Hamilton, Neil Martin, Jim Scott, Colin Stein, Peter Marinello and Peter Cormack, the club failed to rediscover past glories on the domestic front.

Then, in July 1971, the fiercely grim-faced Eddie Turnbull thundered through the doors of Easter Road and a new era of greatness began. It would last for about four seasons, as Hibs played some of the best football in Scotland and reached five Cup Finals in the process. Even today the names of Hibernian's line-up for 1972/73 reads like a much-loved litany: Herriot, Brownlie, Schaedler; Stanton, Black, Blackley; Edwards, O'Rourke, Gordon, Cropley and Duncan.

This volume is a pictorial account of Hibernian's first 100 years and is a tribute to star players and major triumphs of yesteryear.

'Such stuff as memories are made of.'

Paul Lunney
January 2001

Acknowledgements

I would like to thank the following for their assistance in making this book possible: Stuart Marshall from Collectors' World, Derek Taylor and Raymond Taylor of Kollectables in Glasgow, the *Sunday Mail*, the *Scottish Daily Express*, Jack Murray, David Crotty and everyone at Tempus Publishing, especially James Howarth.

One
The Early Years
(1875-1900)

The Hibs team of 1876. From left to right, back row: P. Hall, O. Quinn, T. Gilhooley, T. Beveridge, J. Candlin, F. Rourke, J. Creamer, M. McGrath. Middle row: M. Byrne, W. Donnelly, M. Whelahan (captain), A. Hughes, D. Browne, J. Keegan. Front row: J. Meechan, A. Watson, T. Flynn.

Hibernian FC, around 1879.

Trophies presented to Hibs by the Edinburgh FA for being the outright winners of the first ever Edinburgh Cup and the Second XI Cup in three successive years – 1879, 1880 and 1881.

Weaving wonder and prankster, 'Darling' Willie Groves was the subject of an SFA inquiry before Hibs won the Scottish Cup in 1887. Semi-final victims Vale of Leven lodged a protest that Groves had received illegal payments from Hibs. The verdict was not proven, but only on the casting vote of SFA President Mr Brown. Born at Leith on 9 November 1869, Willie joined the Green Jerseys from Leith Harp in February 1886 and moved to Celtic in August 1888. An apprentice shoe-finisher in Gorgie, Groves became one of the finest footballers ever to play the game. A breathtaking dribbler and precision passer, he won League and Cup honours with West Bromwich Albion and Aston Villa, and was capped three times for Scotland (scoring a hat-trick against Ireland in his second game). In 1894, his health collapsed with the onset of tuberculosis and, although he played in the 1896 Scottish Cup final, his career ended at Rushden two years later. Willie was working as a labourer for Edinburgh Corporation by the end of 1903 and he died in utter penury in February 1908.

Dashing attacker Tom Maley made his Hibernian debut in a 2-1 Scottish Cup quarter-final win over Third Lanark on Christmas Day 1886. During his career, the teams he played for included Partick Thistle, Third Lanark and Celtic. As manager he guided Manchester City to FA Cup glory in 1904, but was suspended in 1906 (lifted in 1910) for awarding bonuses under the counter. In his defence, most clubs were doing exactly the same thing around this time. A headmaster and fine platform lecturer, his brothers Willie (Celtic) and Alec (Hibs) were excellent managers in their own right.

Scheming inside forward Mick Dunbar scored four times for the Hibees in a 6-0 thrashing of Hearts in the Roseberry Charity Cup semi-final at Powderhall on 14 April 1888. The following month he played in Celtic's inaugural match and subsequently became a director of the Glasgow club. Capped for Scotland against Ireland in 1886, Dunbar became a successful wine and spirit merchant. His brother Tom played for Celtic and the Scottish League.

Although James Kelly's name is more synonymous with Renton and Celtic, he did help out Hibernian from time to time. When four Green Greats were selected to play for Edinburgh against Renfrewshire on 16 October 1886, Kelly was drafted into the side to face St Bernards. The star international pivot celebrated his Hibs debut by scoring twice in a 5-2 win. Having made a number of appearances at Easter Road early in 1888, Kelly gave a verbal agreement that he would join the club the next season (1888/89) on a permanent basis. However, the birth of Celtic put paid to that idea. In later life Kelly was a publican, county councillor and JP.

Hibs in 1887. From left to right, back row: Tom Maley, James McGhee (captain), John McFadden (club secretary), Peter McGinn, Paddy McGovern, Phil Clarke. Middle row: Robert McGeachan (assistant secretary), Tommy Lee, John Tobin, James McLaren, Owen Brannigan, Willie Groves. Front row: James Lundie, George Smith, Sandy McMahon.

James McGhee was captain of the Scottish Cup-winning side of 1887, and a member of the fabulous half-back line of McGhee, McGinn and McLaren. They were the Three Musketeers, always ready for the cut and thrust of a game. McGhee and colleague Jimmy Lundie were the first Hibs players to be capped, in a 4-1 victory over Wales in Glasgow on 10 April 1886. McGhee went over to Celtic only upon the demise of Hibernian around Christmas 1890. Not surprisingly, he was an unpopular choice as Hearts manager with the Tynecastle supporters in 1908. Things came to a head with a controversial suspension of Bobby Walker, late in 1909. Jimmy left for Philadelphia, USA where he died, around 1945.

One of the most bewildering dribblers and powerful ball-headers of his time, Sandy McMahon joined Celtic along with Jimmy McGhee in late 1890. A regular in the Hibernian line-up since January 1889, McMahon went on to win 6 caps for Scotland, including three consecutive fixtures against England in 1892, 1893 and 1894. Nicknamed 'Duke' after the Duc de Mac-Mahon, President of France from 1873 to 1879, Sandy ended his career with Partick Thistle in 1904 and died in Glasgow on 25 January 1916.

Personality forward Phil Clarke's equalizing strike in the 1887 Scottish Cup final against Dumbarton at Hampden Park spurred the Green Jerseys on to silver success. Clarke made a goalscoring debut for Hibs in a 3-2 away win over Partick Thistle on 16 February 1884, and subsequently became a mainstay of the side. Injured in a friendly challenge match versus Aston Villa, the Hibees met Rangers in a benefit game on 1 June 1887 to help ease his financial worries. Phil went to the short-lived Glasgow Hibernian on loan in 1889.

Dan Doyle, the best back of the 1890s.

Irrepressible Dan Doyle was an unashamed football 'soldier of fortune'. Born in Paisley on 16 September 1864, this powerfully-built, curly-haired giant had it all. A handsome and humorous all-round athlete, Doyle made his Hibernian debut at Airdrie in aid of striking Lanarkshire coal miners on 19 March 1887. Hibs won the match 5-3. After a brief interlude with East Stirlingshire he returned to play against Rangers in August 1888, but his itchy feet had seen him star for Newcastle East End, Grimsby, Bolton and Everton before settling in Glasgow with Celtic. Capped on 8 occasions for Scotland (5 of which were against England) Dan Doyle was a charismatic personality – a true maverick.

A talented forward of considerable craft and skill, Jimmy Blessington joined Hibernian from Harp Athletic in 1889. Born at Linlithgow on 28 February 1874, he was the son of a quarryman, but abandoned his apprenticeship as a blacksmith to join Celtic in August 1892 from Leith Athletic. Blessington gained 4 full caps (which included a superb performance in Scotland's 2-1 victory over England in 1894) and made 5 Scottish League appearances. He played for a number of English clubs around the turn of the century and became Leicester Fosse's first manager in July 1907. In 1913 he was appointed coach to Belfast Celtic and also served as an athletics handicapper under the Irish AAA. Latterly, he was a licensee in the Devonshire town of Newton Abbot, where he died on 18 April 1939.

HIBERNIAN FOOTBALL CLUB
· 1894 - 1895 ·

The Hibernian team which won the first two seasons of the Scottish League Division Two Championship in the 1893/94 and 1894/95 seasons.

The Hibs team around the 1894/95 season.

Postcard of the Hibs, *c.* 1900.

The team which reached the 1896 Scottish Cup final at Logie Green. Captain Bernie Breslin is holding the ball.

Action from the 1896 Scottish Cup final at Logie Green against Hearts. Notice that the goalkeeper is recognisable only by the fact that he is wearing a cap. Distinctive jerseys for 'keepers were not introduced until 1909.

The attendance for the Logie Green final fell around 3,000 short of the 20,000 capacity because of fears concerning the safety of the ground. Hearts won 3-1, with O'Neill scoring Hibs' only goal of the game.

The Scotland side that played against Ireland in Belfast on 30 January 1897. It contained four Hibs players. Scotland won 2-0. The full side was, from left to right, back row: W.G. Andrew (Dundee), J. Kennedy (Hibs), N. Smith (Rangers), J.H. McLaughlin (Celtic), President A. Raisbeck (Hibs), T. McFarlane (Hibs), trainer J.J. Mullen (Celtic). Middle row: D.R. Montgomery (Third Lanark), Hon. Treasurer P. Murray (Hibs), J. Miller (Rangers), James Kelly (Celtic), N. Gibson (Rangers), A. Smith (Rangers), A. Towns (St Mirren), vice-president H. Farr (Abercorn). Front row: C. Traynor (Abercorn), A. King (Celtic).

Alongside fellow Scotland international Patrick Murray, John Kennedy was part of an exceptional Hibs right-wing. He came into the side in 1893 as another product of the prolific Broxburn Shamrock. After being promoted to the top division in 1895, Kennedy scored a hat-trick in consecutive League games against Dumbarton and Hearts. The Murray/Kennedy partnership had a telepathic understanding, with their rapid interchanging of positions bewildering the opposition. John Kennedy moved to Stoke in March 1898 and then to Glossop at the turn of the century. He was capped against Wales in 1897.

Edinburgh lad Paddy Murray was a player with St Patrick's CYMS and Campsie before joining the resurrected Hibernian in February 1893. From the outside-right position Murray was an excellent team man, who became a brilliant maker and taker of scoring opportunities. Capped for Scotland on two occasions, he retired in 1901, when Hibs rewarded him with a benefit match against Celtic. Murray died on Christmas Day 1925. His son later starred for Falkirk, during the 1920s.

Two
Cup Winners and Champions
(1900-1919)

The Scottish League Champions of 1902/03.

It is not often that Hibs have held both the Scottish Cup and the League Championship. Early in 1903 they did, along with the Glasgow Charity Cup, the Rosebery Cup and the Macrae Cup. The successful committee and players are pictured above. From left to right, back row: P. Cannon, C. Carolan, P. Smith, A. McPhee, O. Brannigan, D. McMichael, F. Rennie, B. Lester, J. Pollock, Mr Brandon. Third row: J. Buchan, J. Hogg, A. Gray, R. Glen, H. Handling, J. Divers. Second row: J. Stewart, B. Breslin, J. Harrower, R. Atherton, A. Robertson, J. McColl, H.G. Rennie. Front row: P. Callaghan, W. McCartney.

A ball artist with a tremendous work rate, Johnny Divers joined Hibs from Celtic in November 1901 and finished the season as the club's top scorer in all competitions, with 12 goals. Earlier in his career, on 28 October 1896, he, Peter Meechan and Barney Battles had refused to play against Hibs in a vital League match unless certain reporters were removed from the press box. Celtic took a high moral line: the trio were suspended, had their wages cut drastically and were eventually transferred. Divers scored in his only international appearance for Scotland, against Wales, on 23 March 1895. In the 1902 Scottish Cup final he was given the specialist role of stopping Celt Sandy McMahon jumping at corners.

Cartoon depicting the 1902 'Battle of the Greens' Scottish Cup final at Celtic Park. Hibs won 1-0 through a backheeled goal from Andy McGeachan. The Hibs line-up was as follows: Rennie, Gray, Glen, Breslin, Harrower, Robertson, McColl, McGeachan, Divers, Callaghan and Atherton.

ST. HIBERNIAN AND THE DRAGON.

The Monster of the North Conquered at Last.

Cartoon depicting Hibs' 1-0 victory over Dundee at Easter Road on 27 September 1902. It ended the Dens Park club's six successive wins since the opening day of the season. Hibs marched on to take the 1902/03 League Championship title, recording only one defeat (0-1 versus Third Lanark) in the process.

Comic strip of Hibs' 0-0 Scottish Cup third round replay draw with Dundee in 1903. The Tayside team won the second replay at Ibrox 1-0.

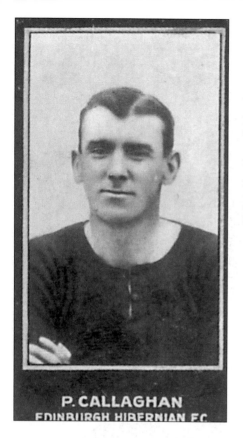

P. CALLAGHAN
EDINBURGH HIBERNIAN F.C.

Douglas Lamming's excellent *Who's Who of Scottish Internationalists* says of Paddy Callaghan: 'Inside left but in his long service with Hibs filled many positions including several outings in goal. Known as an "artful dodger on the ball" and for having "a reputation of clean and gentlemanly play".' Born in Glasgow on 12 August 1879, Callaghan joined Hibernian from Jordanhill in 1898 and made his Easter Road debut the following year. His one cap for Scotland came on 3 March 1900 in a 3-0 win over Ireland in Belfast. A consistent performer and wonderful club servant, Callaghan was a Glasgow licensee between the wars and died on 26 February 1959.

Outside left Bobby Atherton was born in Wales on 29 July 1876, but moved to Scotland as a child. Educated in Edinburgh, he played for Dalry Primrose and Hearts before transferring to Hibernian in 1898. Captain of the team which won the Cup in 1902 and League in 1903, he fancied himself as a vocalist and gave a rendition of *Dolly Gray* after being presented with the Scottish Cup. Speedy, with an artistic style of play, he moved to Middlesbrough in May 1903, and won 9 caps for Wales (5 while a Hibee). He retired to work as a commercial traveller for a firm of office suppliers, but was killed during the First World War when the submarine he was serving on was lost in the English Channel in November 1917.

ATHERTON.

OGDEN'S CIGARETTES

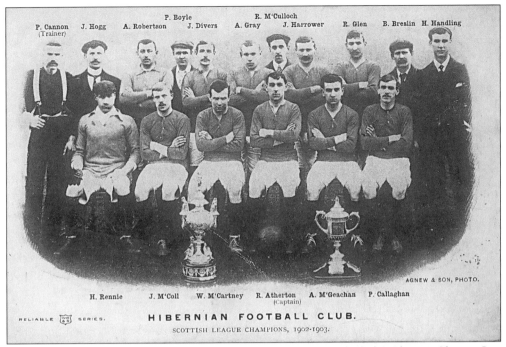

P. Cannon (Trainer) J. Hogg A. Robertson P. Boyle J. Divers A. Gray R. M'Culloch J. Harrower R. Glen B. Breslin H. Handling

AGNEW & SON, PHOTO.

H. Rennie J. M'Coll W. M'Cartney R. Atherton (Captain) A. M'Geachan P. Callaghan

RELIABLE SERIES.

HIBERNIAN FOOTBALL CLUB.

SCOTTISH LEAGUE CHAMPIONS, 1902-1903.

The great Hibs team of the 1902/03 season. The trophies pictured are the Glasgow Charity Cup and the Scottish Cup.

Sturdy little right-half Barney Breslin joined Hibs from his local club Carfin Shamrock in 1893. A consistent and loyal Hibee who had a genial good temper, Breslin's lack of speed was amply atoned for by energetic tackling and rare judgement. He was a member of the Second (1894/95) and First Division (1902/03) championship squads and played in the Cup Final sides of 1896 and 1902. Capped against Wales in 1897, he died from a fatal disease in November 1913, aged thirty-nine.

B. Breslin Captain

The Hibernian team of 1906/07, from left to right, back row: W. Duguid, T. Connelly, J. Hogg, J. Adams, J. Main, W. McNeill, J. Gordon, J. Maconnachie (captain), H. McCann, G. Dalrymple, R. Lawrie. Front row: T. Findlay, P. Callaghan, J. Harrower, H.G. Rennie, J. Grieve.

A quiet moment from a Falkirk v. Hibs match, 1900s.

Cigarette card depicting Hibs' ace forward Paddy Callaghan.

Postcard of Hibernian given out by the magazine *Ideas*, *c.* 1909. From left to right, back row: P. Cannon (trainer), J. Weir, S. Allan, W.R. Allan, T.A. Birrell, W. Smith, J.H. Sharp. Middle row: J. Main, J. Edgar, M. Paterson, W. Duguid, J. Peggie, P. Callaghan. Front row: D.M.K. Dixon, J. O'Hara.

Born at West Calder, Midlothian on 29 May 1886, right-back James Main was a stout and resolute defender who signed for Hibs from Junior football in 1904. In a League match against Partick Thistle at Firhill on Christmas Day 1909, Main tackled Frank Branscombe, the Thistle winger, and collapsed on the treacherous and frostbound pitch. His team-mates took him home, but after a sleepless night he was admitted into the Royal Infimary where he had an emergency operation for a suspected ruptured bowel. He never recovered and died of internal injuries on 29 December 1909. Main was capped in a 5-0 win over Ireland at Ibrox on 15 March 1909, and also represented the Scottish League against the Football League in 1908.

Goalkeeper Willie Allan played in East Stirlingshire's first ever Second Division game on 18 August 1900 against Airdrieonians. He was also the first player to be transferred from Falkirk after they became members of the Scottish League, when he joined Rangers for a fee of £100 in December 1903. After returning to Falkirk he took over from the legendary Harry Rennie at Easter Road in 1908, and starred in the 1914 Scottish Cup final.

Memorial card for Hibernian's superb right-back James Main.

WM. ALLAN,
Hibernian F.C.

Portrait of Willie Allan, Hibernian's safe custodian from 1908 to 1916. At 6 ft and 12 st. 4 lb, he struck a redoubtable figure between the posts. An all-round sportsman, Allan was also a keen singer.

Left-sided winger Willie Smith was a tantalizing tormentor of defences the length and breadth of Scotland. He came into the Hibs side in 1908 and immediately set hearts racing with his individual wizardry and accurate crosses. Smith notched up a hat-trick against Dundee in a League match on 25 January 1913, and also netted Hibs' consolation goal in the 1-4 Scottish Cup final replay reverse at the hands of Celtic the following year.

A Scottish League internationalist on three occasions, his benefit game was against Rangers on Christmas Day, 1913.

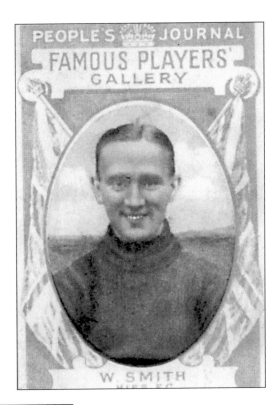

Speedy, top class outside right forward George Rae arrived at Easter Road in 1910 from East Stirlingshire. Rae led the Ibrox defence a merry dance when Hibernian slaughtered Rangers 5-0 on 6 January 1912, and scored two of the goals himself. A contemporary appraisal said Geordie 'dribbles beautifully, centres accurately, and shoots with considerable force'.

J. LAMB,
Hibernian F.C.

Irishman Johnny Lamb signed for Hibernian from Kirkintilloch Rob Roy in the autumn of 1909, and was drafted into the side on that fateful Christmas Day when Jimmy Main met with his injury. Born in County Armagh, Lamb was a tall, well-built, long-striding left half, who had the strength to look after himself on the football field. Called up for an Ireland international in 1912, he was unfortunate not to be selected to play.

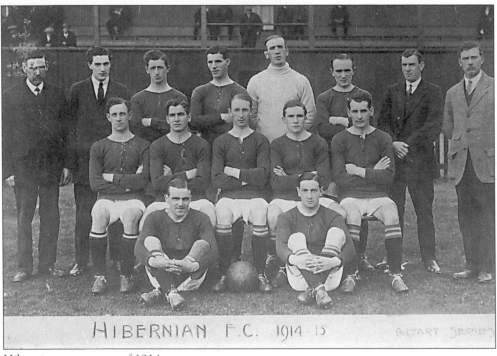

HIBERNIAN F.C. 1914-15

Hibernian team group of 1914.

N. GIRDWOOD,

Popular full-back Neil Girdwood came from Law and joined Hibernian in 1910. The joker in the Hibs pack, he was not averse to giving an opponent the odd sly trip or nudge when the referee had his back turned. At 5 ft 9 in and 12 st 11 lb, Girdwood was a solid defender and fine footballer who made up for his lack of speed with judicious judgement in the tackle.

Hibs players relax with a game of golf at Gullane in preparation for the 1914 Scottish Cup final.

Bobby Templeton clears the danger from Celts centre forward Ebenezer Owers in the Scottish Cup final of 1914.

Willie Allan safely clutches the ball from Celtic's Englishman Owers during the 1914 final at Ibrox.

A newspaper artist's impression of the first Scottish Cup final game, which ended goal-less. Celtic won the replay 4-1.

Hibernian Football Club, Scottish Cup final team, April 1914. From left to right, top row: Matt Paterson (captain and centre half), N. Girdwood (right-back), R. Templeton (left-back). Second row: A.R. Grosert (left half-back), P. Kerr (right half-back), W. Smith (outside left). Third row: W. Allen (goalkeeper), R. Wilson (outside right), S. Fleming (inside right). Bottom row: J. Hendren (centre forward), J. Wood (inside left).

Three
Between the Wars
(1919-1939)

HIBERNIANS FOOTBALL CLUB—Season 1921-22.

Players—Left to Right—Back—Maley, Dornan, Ritchie, Harper, Shaw, Christopher.
Front—Kerr, Dunn, Halligan, Paterson, McGinnigle, Walker, Young

Most of the men who took Hibs to the Scottish Cup finals of 1923 and 1924.

Midfield maestro and practical joker Jimmy Dunn cost Hibs only £20 from St Anthony's during the summer of 1920. Born in Glasgow on 25 November 1900, 'Ginger' was the Billy Bremner of his day, a hard-working skilled performer who packed a thunderous shot which belied his slight frame of 5 ft 6 in and 10 st. 7 lb. Hibernian's top scorer in both the 1924/25 and 1925/26 seasons, Dunn moved to Everton along with Harry Ritchie after Scotland beat England 5-1 at Wembley in 1928.

Hibs defender Hugh Shaw clears from Celt Patsy Gallagher during the 1923 Scottish Cup final at Hampden Park. Celtic won 1-0.

Action from the 1924 Scottish Cup final at Ibrox. Hibs defenders – from left to right, Dornan, Shaw, Dunn, Miller and McGinnigle – can only watch in despair as Russell of Airdrie places his header past Harper to open the scoring. Airdrie won 2-0.

Like Dunn, striker Jimmy McColl originally made his name with St Anthony's. He netted the ball twice against Hibs in the 1914 Scottish Cup final replay and was a consistent goalscorer for Celtic throughout the war. He undoubtedly would have won Scotland honours had internationals been played at that time. McColl cost Stoke City £2,250 in May 1920, but he was homesick in the Potteries and returned to Partick Thistle in 1921 before moving across the country to Edinburgh the following year. In 1971, Hibernian presented him with a gold watch to mark his fifty years' service to the club as player, trainer and general assistant. The first man to score 100 League and cup goals for Hibs, he died in 1978 aged eighty-five.

Cartoon of Hibernian's 1924 Scottish Cup final defeat by Airdrieonians.

The Hibs team of 1923/24. From left to right, back row: Dornan, Shaw, Harper, Miller. Middle row: Ritchie, McColl, Kerr, Walker, McGinnigle. Front row: Halligan, Dunn.

The Hibees' 'Wembley Wizard', Jimmy Dunn played in both the 1923 and 1924 Scottish Cup finals. A junior, full and Scottish League internationalist, 'Ginger' won League Division Two (1931), Division One (1932) and FA Cup (1933) winners' medals with Everton, where he had a perfect understanding with the legendary centre forward Dixie Dean. The life and soul of the dressing-room, he sadly died of cancer on 20 August 1963, aged sixty-two.

Willie Harper was arguably Hibs' greatest ever goalkeeper. He played for Broxburn St Andrews, Winchburgh Thistle and Edinburgh Emmet before signing for Davy Gordon in 1920. During the First World War, he served with the Scots Guards (becoming the Brigade's rugby and boxing champion) and then the Royal Flying Corps as an aircraftsman. In November 1925, he joined Arsenal for a then record fee for a goalkeeper of £4,500. He subsequently played in America for Fall River and Boston, and served Plymouth Argyle for over fifty years as player, trainer, groundsman and backroom helper. A former blacksmith, Bill won 9 Scotland caps while at Easter Road and died in April 1989 aged ninety-two.

Tall left half Hugh Shaw joined Hibs in 1918. A big man and a skillful footballer, he had the ability to switch play and was seldom flustered under pressure. Shaw became the club's trainer in 1937, and as manager from 1947/48 guided them to three League championships in the 1947/48, 1950/51 and 1951/52 seasons. He resigned in November 1961 and took charge of Raith Rovers.

A native of Newhaven, centre forward Peter Flucker joined Hibs in 1932, and helped the Easter Road men take the 1932/33 Division Two championship. The following season, Peter celebrated Hibernian's return to the top flight by finishing the year as their leading League scorer with 12 goals. On 23 January 1935, he hit all five of Hibs' goals in their 5-0 Scottish Cup win over Vale of Atholl. A man of many clubs, Flucker also played for Mussleburgh Brutonians, Hearts, Arbroath, Queen of the South and St Bernards.

This is the Hibs side for 1933/34, the club's first season back in the top division after winning the 1932/33 Division Two title. From left to right, back row: Langton, Wilkinson, Blyth, Urquhart, Watson, Crawford. Front row: Walls, Wallace, Halligan, Flucker, Somerville.

Perth-born goalkeeper George Blyth came into the Hibs side in January 1930 when regular custodian Robb dislocated a finger. Signed from Fifeshire Junior team Newburgh West End, Blyth broke a leg in a Division Two game against St Bernards in the 1931/32 season. However, he made a full recovery and his confident hands and sureness of eye helped Hibs back into the top flight in 1933.

Centre half Willie Watson signed for Hibs from junior team Stoneyburn in 1930. Watson immediately made a name for himself in senior football with a great display against McGrory of Celtic. A fine figure of a man in his playing days, it was said that 'he would happily impersonate Rob Roy with his red locks and air of daring resistance'. He won a League cap against the Irish in September 1933, but was given a free transfer after a poor performance against Hearts on 21 September 1935. He moved to Ayr United and then Lincoln City.

Hibs concede a goal to Hearts – Black scrambles the ball over the line, while Watson and the 'keeper vainly try to hook it away.

P. WILSON

Cool, creative and stylish right half Peter Wilson joined Hibs from Celtic in August 1934. Born in Beith in 1905, he had won League, cup and international honours at Parkhead before coming to Easter Road. Peter perfected his passing ability into such a fine art that he was said to stroke the ball, not merely kick it. Wilson became Dunfermline's manager in 1938, and later scouted for Derby County.

Cleland-born Tommy Egan moved to senior football from Wishaw Juniors in 1934. He started playing at Easter Road as outside left, but an injury to a team-mate saw him posted to the left half position. Tommy had excellent ball control and his good distribution was a great asset to the side. At inside forward he scored a hat-trick against Clyde on 18 September 1937.

T. EGAN

A tall, quiet and unassuming lad when he arrived at Parkhead in 1923, Peter Wilson emerged as a wonderful wing-half. Red-faced, with laughing eyes, Peter also had bigger ears than most people. 'They catch so much wind they cost me a yard in speed', he used to say. In his final appearance for Scotland against England in 1933, he started the move which led to the winning goal scored by Jimmy McGrory, and the 'Hampden Roar' was born. Peter Wilson died in his native Beith on 13 February 1983. Like a true Ayrshireman, he was a great Burns enthusiast and performer.

Outside left J. Borland arrived at Easter Road in the summer of 1934 from Shawfield Juniors. A strongly-built youth, Borland was never a regular first-team choice as he vied with Allison over the the wing position. He was released in the 1937/38 season.

William Bryson was an excellent left-back who gave good service to Morton Juniors before joining Hibernian. He was a schoolteacher by profession.

Glasgow-born forward Tommy Brady (left) and Irish internationalist Jack Jones (right). Brady joined Hibs from Wishaw Juniors in 1935 and finished the 1935/36 season as the club's top League scorer with 18 goals. He moved to Aberdeen in 1938.

Captain and Irish international centre half Jack Jones (left) signed for Hibs from Linfield in December 1935 for an Irish and Hibs record transfer fee of £5,000 (apparently financed by an Edinburgh bookmaker), in their efforts to fight off relegation. Goalkeeper Gourley (right) signed from Partick Thistle in 1937. A product of Dunipace, he had previously spent a loan period with Albion Rovers.

Falkirk-born right-back Alexander Prior joined Hibernian from Partick Thistle in 1937.

TALE OF A SPIDER AT EASTER ROAD

Cartoon of Hibs' 3-2 League win over Clyde on 19 August 1939. Two weeks later war broke out and caused the League programme to be abandoned.

Wee centre forward Arthur Milne (5ft 5in) was Hibernian's top goalscorer in both the 1937/38 and 1938/39 seasons. Hibs' manager was quick to notice that he had gone to Liverpool from Dundee United in March 1937 on trial but was not on the retained list of either, and swooped to sign him. Liverpool were ordered to pay £750 compensation to United over the mix-up; however, this was of little consolation to the Tayside men as they had lost a prolific scorer. A native of Brechin, Milne played for local side Victoria before going to Tannadice, and scored a record 4 goals on his Dundee United debut. He scored around 100 goals for Hibs, two of which came in the wartime 8-1 victory over Rangers.

Four
McCartney's Boys to Men
(1939-1949)

Hibs team of 1944. From left to right, back row: Finnigan, Hall, Kean, Downie, Baxter, Shaw, Bogan. Front row: Smith, Milne, McCartney (manager), Nutley, Caskie.

The impeccably-dressed Hibernian manager Willie McCartney had been the boss of rivals Hearts for sixteen years until falling out with the Tynecastle directors in 1935. He took over the post at the other end of the city twelve months later. McCartney had the happy knack of convincing the best youngsters in the country that their futures lay at Easter Road; indeed, he stole Gordon Smith right from under Hearts' nose. On 24 January 1948, during a Scottish Cup tie against Albion Rovers at Cliftonhill, the big man collapsed and died later that night. Hibs had lost a charismatic personality and the man responsible for pushing them to the forefront in Scottish football. A memorial match was played in his honour against FA Cup holders Manchester United in September 1948.

Brilliant young goalkeeper Jimmy Kerr arrived at Easter Road from Ormiston Primrose in November 1938. Tall and well built, Kerr served six years in the Forces. After being demobbed, he gave many fine displays and was consistently in the running for international honours. Jimmy eventually moved to Queen of the South, where he did not play long because he broke his leg in a domestic accident. He went on Hibs' board of directors during the 1970/71 season.

KEAN

Whole-hearted half-back Sammy Kean joined Hibernian from Kirkintilloch Rob Roy during the 1936/37 season as a forward. In December 1938, Hibs turned down a £10,000 offer from Manchester United for him and Tommy McIntyre. At Easter Road Kean transferred from left-wing to left half and soon starred in that position. A Summer Cup winner in 1941, he also played in the 1947 Scottish Cup final and won a 1947/48 League Championship medal.

Signed by Hibernian from Juvenile club Inveresk Thistle, inside right Bobby Combe made an excellent debut in senior football, scoring a goal in Hibs' 5-3 win over Hearts at Tynecastle in April 1941. He topped that feat later that same year by scoring four times against Rangers in the famous 8-1 game. Combe moved back to wing half with the emergence of the Famous Five, and gained success as skipper with League Championship medals in 1948, 1951 and 1952. A loyal Hibee, he spent all his senior playing days at Easter Road, enjoying sixteen years of consistency – with 354 peacetime matches and 67 goals. Combe retired in June 1957 and was appointed as Hibs' assistant trainer before becoming Dunfermline's first full-time manager in 1959.

Born at Annathill on 5 May 1917, Davie Shaw was a grand, intelligent left-back. Signed from Grange Rovers in 1939, Davie and elder brother Jock of Rangers set a record by being the first brothers ever to form the back division in a Scottish international team, when Scotland beat England 1-0 at Hampden Park in April 1946. Davie Shaw also captained Hibs in the 1947 Scottish Cup final. He moved to the Granite City on 15 July 1950, and immediately became the Dons' skipper. Shaw served Aberdeen loyally in three different capacities, as player, trainer and manager.

Left half Sammy Kean represented Scotland in a wartime international against England in 1943 and was also selected for the Scottish League in their 7-3 win over the Irish on 30 April 1947.

Captain Combe was a schoolboy, League and full Scottish international player. Leith-born and bred, he became a shopkeeper in that area and was subsequently employed in the marketing department of the Scottish Gas board.

Scotland and Scottish League internationalist Davie Shaw won a 1947/48 Championship medal with Hibs. Known as 'Faither' by the players, he retired as Aberdeen's trainer in 1967 and died in 1977.

Mining Engineer Jock Govan joined Hibs from his local Larkhall Thistle in 1942. At Easter Road he formed a formidable full-back partnership with Davie Shaw, and represented Scotland on six occasions. The first of the overlapping full-backs, Govan won three League Championship medals with Hibernian before moving on to Ayr United in 1954. He died in Edinburgh on 19 February 1999.

Ticket stub for Hibs' 2-0 Summer Cup win over Celtic in 1945.

Scottish Football Association
LIMITED

SUMMER CUP—SEMI-FINAL TIE

CELTIC
v.
HIBERNIAN

TYNECASTLE PARK
EDINBURGH

Stand "B" (North) 4/6
(Including Tax)

SATURDAY, 23rd JUNE 1945
Kick-off 3 p.m.

Row Q   Seat

This Ticket to be retained by Holder
GEO. G. GRAHAM, Secretary

Enter by Turnstile No. 28 or 29

HUGH
HOWIE
HIBERNIAN

Born in Glasgow on St Valentine's Day 1924, Hugh Howie arrived at Easter Road in 1943 from Newton Juniors. A fine utility player, Howie was fielded in all defensive positions and always performed skilfully. He scored in his only international appearance for Scotland, a 3-1 win over Wales on 23 October 1948. Howie came back bravely following a long illness, but retired on medical grounds in 1954. He took up journalism when he left the game and sadly met an early death in a motor accident on 14 January 1958.

Outside right Gordon Smith joined Hibs from Dundee North End in April 1941. Smith had incredible ball control and centering ability and graced any game with his elegant style of play. He scored over 300 goals in Scottish senior football between 1941 and 1964 and won 18 Scotland caps. Non-smoker Smith adopted a strict attitude towards his health during his career, eating mainly fresh fruit and salads and rarely drinking alcohol, tea or coffee.

Matchday programme for the 1946 Victory Cup final. Johnny Aitkenhead scored Hibs' goal in the 3-1 defeat. The Hibernian team was: Kerr, Govan, Shaw, Howie, Aird, Finnigan, Smith, Peat, Milne, Aitkenhead, Nutley.

AIRD

Red-haired Peter Aird was a terrier of a half-back who knew the value of precise passing. He played in the 1947 Scottish Cup final and won a League Championship medal the following year.

TURNBULL

Robust inside left Eddie Turnbull was born in Falkirk on 12 April 1923, and signed for Hibs from Forth Rangers of Grangemouth in 1946. A non-stop competitor, Turnbull was a tough-tackling, rampaging forward with an explosive shot. He hung up his boots in 1959 to become club trainer, latterly in charge at Queen's Park and Aberdeen before returning to Easter Road to mould one of the finest Hibs sides in the club's history.

Nicknamed 'The Gay Gordon' in the relatively innocent early 1950s, Gordon Smith was a majestic sight in full flow, running down the right wing for Hibs. Born in Edinburgh on 24 May 1924, the son of a Montrose grocer, Gordon won schoolboy, Scottish League and full international honours. He established two records: winning League Championship medals with three different clubs (Hibs, Hearts and Dundee), and a Scottish League winger's highest score (five goals against Third Lanark on 8 November 1947). Smith also starred in the European Cup for this trio of clubs and won Scotland's Player of the Year award in 1951.

Programme for the 1947 Scottish Cup final. Johnny Cuthbertson gave Hibs a first-minute lead in the 2-1 defeat by Aberdeen. The Hibernian team was: Kerr, Govan, Shaw, Howie, Aird, Kean, Smith, Finnigan, Cuthbertson, Turnbull and Ormond.

Captains Frank Dunlop of Aberdeen and Hibee Davie Shaw shake hands before the kick-off.

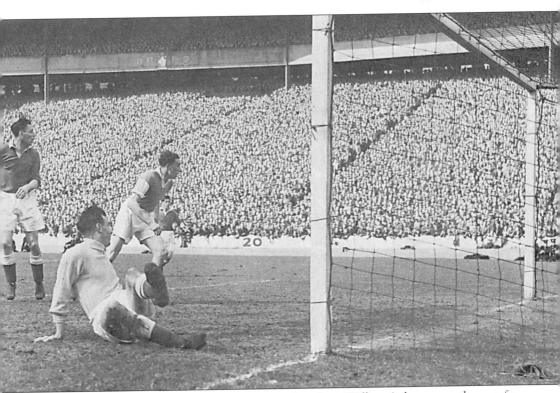
Goalkeeper Kerr looks round in despair to see striker Stan Williams' shot enter the net for Aberdeen's winning goal.

The reverse side of Hibernian's 1947/48 Scottish League Championship medal.

The Hibs squad that captured the Championship trophy in 1948.

Five

Five go to Town
(1949-1959)

'Last Minute' Lawrie Reilly, Hibernian's most-capped player and greatest goalscorer. Born in Edinburgh on 28 October 1928, he arrived at Easter Road in 1945 via Merchiston, Murrayfield Athletic and Edinburgh Thistle. Originally signed as a right-winger, Reilly developed into a top-class centre forward. He often appeared at outside left for Scotland and is best remembered for the goals he scored against England – 6 in his first 5 internationals.

The Championship-winning team of the 1950/51 season. From left to right, back row: Howie, Paterson, Younger, Shaw (manager), Govan, Gallagher, Buchanan. Front row: McColl (trainer), Combe, Johnstone, Smith, Reilly, Turnbull, Ormond.

The 1950/51 League Champions in action.

74

Left: Hibs' 1950/51 League Champions medal. *Right*: The reverse side of Hibs' 1951/52 Champions medal.

The men who won the 1951/52 League title. From left to right, back row: Combe, Howie, Paterson, Younger, Shaw (manager), Govan, Gallagher, Buchanan. Front row: Terris (director), Johnstone, Smith, Swan (chairman), Reilly, Turnbull, Ormond, Hartland (director).

Goalkeeper Tommy Younger punches to clear during the 1950/51 League Cup quarter-final replay at Ibrox against Aberdeen. The match ended level at 1-1. Hibs won the second replay at Hampden Park 5-1 .

TOMMY
YOUNGER
(HIBERNIANS)

JOHN
GOVAN.

(HIBS)

EDDIE
TURNBULL (HIBS)

GORDON SMITH.

(HIBERNIAN)

Four caricatures of Hibernian's star players from the early 1950s.

Capped 38 times for Scotland, despite being physically small at 5 ft 7 in and 10 st 6 lbs, Lawrie Reilly was surprisingly sturdy and a supremely opportunistic attacker. Honoured on a further 13 occasions by the Scottish League, he was a painter and decorator at the beginning of his career and later became a licensee in the Edinburgh area.

Lawrie Reilly

Lawrie Reilly made his Hibernian debut at Rugby Park on 13 October 1945. He was only sixteen years of age, and played in a winning side. It was in 1953 at Wembley that he earned his title 'Last Minute', when he snatched a goal in the ninetieth minute to give Scotland a 2-2 draw. In March 1958, he announced his retirement and ended his career in some style on 21 April 1958 by scoring a goal in a 3-1 win over Rangers at Easter Road.

Matchday programme for the Coronation Cup final in 1953. Hibs lined up as follows: Younger, Govan, Paterson, Buchanan, Howie, Combe, Smith, Johnstone, Reilly, Turnbull, Ormond.

Stand ticket for the Coronation Cup final. Hibs lost 2-0 to Celtic, but it wasn't through lack of skill or effort, as time and again the Famous Five forward line were foiled by Celtic's courageous custodian John Bonnar.

SOUTH (EAST) STAND

ENTER ONLY AT TURNSTILES **B**

SCOTTISH ASSOCIATION FOOTBALL LIMITED

The Coronation Cup, 1953

FINAL TIE

HAMPDEN PARK, GLASGOW

WEDNESDAY, 20th MAY, 1953

Kick-off 7 p.m.

PRICE **7/6**   *G. G. Graham*

Including Tax   Secretary

THIS PORTION TO BE RETAINED   *Row* **E**

Seat No. **70**

Hugh Howie kicks the ball off the line from Jimmy Walsh's shot; unfortunately, it went straight back to the Celt, who smashed it into the net for goal number two.

Willie Ormond challenges Partick Thistle 'keeper Smith for the ball at Firhill.

HIBERNIAN (Winners of Scottish League Division A)—Standing: Combe, Paterson, Govan, Younger, H. Shaw (Manager), Buchanan, Ogilvie Souness, Gallagher. Seated: Smith, Johnstone, Reilly, Turnbull, Ormond.

Autographed teamsheet of Hibernian's 1951/52 Championship squad.

Willie Ormond

Skilful and speedy, outside left William Esplin Ormond came to Edinburgh from Stenhousemuir in November 1946 for a fee of £1,200. A much-injured footballer – his injuries included three broken legs and a fractured arm – he bounced back each time to have a long playing career. Capped for Scotland on 6 occasions, he also represented the Scottish League 10 times. His brother Gibson Ormond played for Airdrieonians.

84

Portrait of Hibernian's wonderful winger Willie Ormond.

Four images of the outrageously talented Gordon Smith. After a short spell with Irish club Drumcondra in 1964, he retired to a quiet life at his North Berwick home.

Two stalwarts of the Scottish team are shown here in opposition. Hibs' centre forward Lawrie Reilly gets above George Young, Rangers' big centre half, to head the ball goalwards. Rangers had a good season and won the Scottish League championship once again. Hibs finished just above halfway in Division One. In this match, played at Ibrox, Rangers beat Hibs 5-3.

Capped on 8 occasions by Scotland, Eddie Turnbull also represented the Scottish League 4 times and played in a B international against England at Dens Park, Dundee on 29 February 1956. The result of the game was a 2-2 draw.

Brilliant Bobby Johnstone was the baby of the Famous Five. Born in the rugby stronghold of Selkirk on 7 September 1929, he joined Hibs from Newtongrange Star in 1946. He was capped 19 times, including six successive internationals against England between 1951 and 1956. Johnstone represented Great Britain against the Rest of Europe in 1955 and was the first man to score in successive FA Cup finals at Wembley with Manchester City, in 1955 and 1956. A superb schemer, he was noted particularly for his precision with the single defence-splitting pass.

Hibs' big blond custodian Tommy Younger joined the club from Hutchison Vale in 1948. Born in Edinburgh on 10 April 1930, he did his National Service with the BAOR and flew home from Germany each weekend to play for Hibernian. Younger cost Liverpool £9,000 in the summer of 1956, and subsequently starred at Falkirk, Stoke City and Leeds United before retiring in October 1962. He was Hibs' PRO in 1969 and chairman Tom Hart brought him onto the board of directors the following year. Tommy Younger was an exceptional goalkeeper, always alert and reliable.

Action shot of Hibs on the attack during the first-leg of the European Cup semi-final against Rheims. Willie Ormond is the player on the right of the picture ready to pounce.

HIBERNIAN F.C. PROGRAMME

Vol. 7   No. 45   **WEDNESDAY, 18th APRIL 1956**   Kick-Off 7.30 p.m.

EUROPEAN CUP   SEMI-FINAL SECOND LEG

Photos by "Scottish Daily Mail"

HIBERNIAN
STADE RHEIMS

6 D

VERSUS

Matchday programme for the European Cup semi-final against Rheims. Hibs lost 1-0 and went out of the competition, 0-3 on aggregate.

Four shots of Gordon Smith in action. A keen golfer and cricket spectator, Gordon was a close friend of the legendary Open Champion Bobby Locke.

Goalkeeper Tommy Younger made 24 consecutive appearances for Scotland, captaining the team on four occasions including two matches in the 1958 World Cup finals, and became the first international footballer to rise to the position of President of the SFA. He died on 13 January 1984.

Centre half Jackie Plenderleith made his League debut twenty-four days after his seventeenth birthday and was thereafter a Hibs regular. Born in Bellshill on 6 October 1937, he came to Easter Road from Ferndale Athletic in1953 and was loaned out to Armadale Thistle. A zealous, unflinching defender, he had an effective understanding with those around him. Plenderleith made 5 appearances for the Under 23 side, and moved to Manchester City for £17,500 in July 1960.

Born at Falkirk on 23 February 1927, after serving Hibs for fifteen years Willie Ormond joined his home town team in August 1961. A masterly dribbler with a terrific shot in his left foot, Willie later became a successful manager of St Johnstone, Hearts, Hibs and Scotland. Awarded an OBE in 1975, he later became a licensee in Musselburgh. He died on 4 May 1984.

Two action shots of Hibernian's centre forward Lawrie Reilly.

Goalie Lawrie Leslie can't stop Celt Sammy Wilson's well-placed header at Parkhead in the 1957/58 season.

Born in the Woolton area of Liverpool (the Beatles' birthplace) on 17 July 1940, of Scottish parents, Joe Baker was raised in Motherwell. A devastating forward, he joined Hibs from Coltness United in 1956 and was loaned out to Armadale Thistle. Scottish schoolboy international Joe was called up to play for England against Northern Ireland by manager Winterbottom in 1959. Baker asked a taxi driver to take him to the England camp's hotel, but when he told the London cabbie, in his broad Scots accent, that he was playing for England, the driver slid his partition shut and radioed for the police! Thankfully, the matter was resolved and Joe scored on his Wembley debut. The Baker boy then moved to Torino, Arsenal, Nottingham Forest and Sunderland, before returning to Easter Road in January 1971. He netted a staggering 16 hat-tricks for Hibs and ended his playing career at Raith Rovers.

Forward Tommy Preston made his mark with Newtongrange Star before being asked along to Easter Road in 1953, an invitation he accepted with alacrity. Tommy's goal incursions and on-target marksmanship made him one of the most feared inside forwards in the country. He netted 4 goals in a 11-1 thrashing of Airdrieonians in the League at Broomfield on 24 October 1959 – Hibs' biggest win to date. Preston played with the club until 1964, and retired to become a publican.

Matchday programme for the 1958 Scottish Cup semi-final against Rangers. The game ended in a 2-2 draw, but Hibs won the replay 2-1 through goals by Turnbull and Fraser.

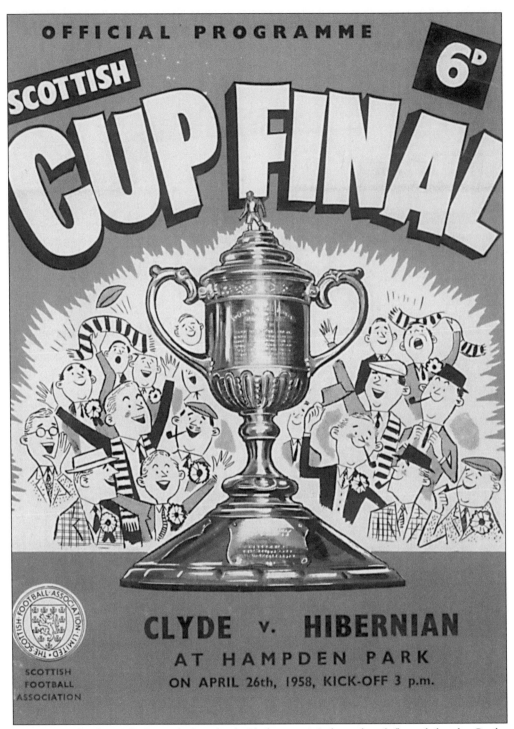

Programme for the 1958 Scottish Cup final. Clyde won 1-0 through a deflected shot by Coyle.

Top: Challenged by Currie of Clyde, Hibernian goalkeeper Leslie loses the ball in the Scottish Cup final. He looks around apprehensively, but the ball ran wide of goal. *Middle and bottom:* Two views of the controversial incident in the final when Hibernian centre forward Baker (number 9) palmed the ball into the goal, with Clyde goalkeeper Murphy out of position. It seemed just as easy for him to have headed the ball.

At either outside right or left, Johnny MacLeod was a handful for any defence. Born in Edinburgh on 23 November 1938, he joined Hibs in 1957 from Armadale Thistle to renew his partnership with Joe Baker and netted twice on his debut in September at Kilmarnock. An all-action, clever manipulator, Johnny always represented a threat with his restless foraging and eagerness to be in the fray. After making 4 appearances for Scotland, he cost Arsenal £40,000 in June 1961. Subsequently, he starred at Aston Villa, Mechelen and Raith Rovers.

Six
Greens Slumber
(1959-1971)

Hibs captain John Fraser shakes hands with Airdrieonians skipper 'Ian' McMillan in the mid-1960s. Fraser joined the club as a right-winger in 1954 from Edinburgh Thistle, and fitted into the Easter Road attacking pattern with pace and sagacity. He later developed into a first-class right-back who was not afraid to venture forward when the opportunity presented itself.

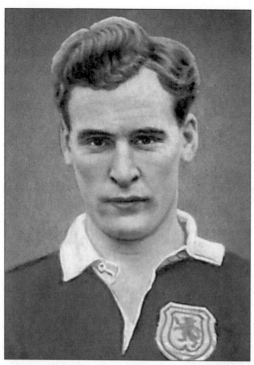

Wing half Sammy Baird cost Hibs £5,000 in October 1960, when he moved from Rangers. The former Scotland international inside forward stayed two years at Easter Road before moving to Third Lanark in November 1962. At 6 ft 1 in and 12 st 8 lbs, Baird was a strong, assertive half-back with a powerful shot. He also played for Clyde, Preston North End and Stirling Albion.

Hibernian FC, 1962/63. From left to right, back row: Gerry Baker, Jim Blair, Bobby Duncan, Willie Wilson, George Seaton, Tom McCready, Alex Cameron, John Grant, Ronnie Simpson, John Byrne, Joe McClelland, Tommy Preston, Duncan Falconer, John Baxter, Joe Easton. Middle row: Ian Cuthbert, Tommy McGlynn, Brian Marjoribanks, Jim O'Rourke, Malcolm Bogie, Doug Logan, Jim Scott, John Fraser, Morris Stevenson, Eric Stevenson. Front row: Bobby Kinloch, George Muir, Pat Hughes, Joe Davis.

Goalkeeper Ronnie Simpson made his debut for Queen's Park at the age of 14 years and 234 days; at the other extreme, he became the oldest player to make a debut for Scotland (aged 36 years and 186 days) in the 3-2 win at Wembley on 15 April 1967. Born in Glasgow on 11 October 1930, the son of Jimmy Simpson of Rangers and Scotland, Ronnie cost Newcastle United £8,750 from Third Lanark in February 1951. He had already played in the 1948 Olympics for Great Britain, and went on to win FA Cup medals with Newcastle in 1952 and 1955. Simpson joined Hibs for £2,000 in October 1960 and departed to Celtic for the same sum four years later. He won a host of honours at Parkhead, including a European Cup winners' medal, and was also voted Scotland's 'Player of the Year' in 1967. Ronnie never played to the gallery and possessed an agility that made difficult shots look easy to save.

One of the finest footballers ever to wear the Green Jersey, Willie Hamilton arrived at Easter Road, from rivals Hearts, in October 1963 for £6,000. Born in Chapelhall on 16 February 1938, he was on the books of Sheffield United and Middlesbrough before moving to Tynecastle. Like many footballing geniuses, Willie was a law unto himself. He was the type who would go on a foreign tour with virtually no luggage, and apparently on one such tour he bent the silver salver 'Man of the Match' award so that it would fit into a small bag. His career was unfortunately hampered with injuries, an ulcer and a drink problem. He cost Aston Villa £25,000 when he left Hibs in August 1965, and also played for Hearts, Ross County and Hamilton Accies before emigrating to Canada, where he died of a heart seizure on 22 October 1976.

Hibernian, 1964/65 season. From left to right, back row: Fraser, Leishman, Wilson, Stanton, McNamee, Stevenson. Front row: O'Rourke, Hamilton, Vincent, Martin, Scott.

The players run a celebratory lap of honour after defeating Real Madrid 2-0 at Easter Road on 7 October 1964. The goalscorers were Cormack and Zoco (own goal). Madrid had participated in the European Cup final only a few months previously, but Jock Stein's Super Hibs side mastered the masters on an unforgettable night.

Small, speedy midfielder Pat Quinn cost Hibernian £26,000 from Blackpool in October 1963. Born in Glasgow on 26 April 1936, Pat was a member of Motherwell's brilliant young team of around 1960, known as the 'Ancell Babes'. Transferred to Blackpool for £34,000 in November 1962, he moved to Easter Road one year later and gave the Hibees excellent service throughout that decade. Subsequently, he was manager of East Fife and assistant to Bertie Auld at both Partick Thistle and Hibernian. Quinn was capped on 4 occasions for Scotland.

Programme for the 1965 Scottish Cup semi-final at Tynecastle, which Dunfermline won 2-0. Future Easter Road favourites Jim Herriot and Alex Edwards were in the 'Pars line-up. The Hibs team consisted of: Wilson, Fraser, Davis, Stanton, McNamee, Baxter, Martin, Quinn, Cormack, Hamilton and Stevenson.

A youthful Peter Cormack stretches for the ball in the 1965 Scottish Cup semi-final at Tynecastle, but is foiled in his effort by Dunfermline's full-back John Lunn and goalkeeper Herriot.

An amusing moment during a Hibs match against Hamilton Accies in the mid-1960s.

Hibernian's defence under pressure from Celtic during the 1965/66 League Cup semi-final at Ibrox. Stanton (Hibs) and McBride (Celtic) look on.

Caricature of the adventurous and intelligent winger Eric Stevenson. Bonnyrigg-born coalminer Eric was a Hearts supporter before joining Hibernian in 1959. 'Stevie' recovered from a badly-broken leg early on in his career, to establish himself as a regular choice in the Hibs line-up. At outside left he possessed a quick change of pace, and blossomed into a rhythmic winger, elegant and ever on the search to kill an opportunity. An ideal club man, Eric represented the Scottish League against the Irish at Ibrox on 19 November 1969.

Full-back and penalty kick specialist Joe Davis made the remarkable record of 273 consecutive appearances for Hibs from late 1964 when he came to Edinburgh from Third Lanark. Originally with Shettleston Juniors, he captained the club for three seasons and his tally of 43 competitive goals was a great credit to his spot kick expertise. A dependable defender, swift in the tackle and quick in recovery, he cleared his perimeter with decisiveness and excellent judgement.

Hibernian, 1968/69 season. From left to right, back row: Jim Brownlee, John Fraser, John Madsen, Ian Wilkinson, Thomson Allan, Willie Wilson, Bobby Duncan, Alan McGraw, Billy Simpson, David Hogg. Middle row: R. Shankly (manager), Pat Stanton, Willie McEwan, Jim Hastie, Peter McCormack, Jim O'Rourke, John Murphy, Colin Grant, John Blackley, George McNeill, T. McNiven (trainer). Front row: Mervyn Jones, Pat Quinn, Morris McCabe, Peter Marinello, Joe Davis, Alex Pringle, Colin Stein, Eric Stevenson.

Matchday programme for the 1968/69 League Cup final.

Thomson Allan punches clear from the danger of Billy McNeill during the 1968/69 League Cup final at Hampden Park. Celtic won 6-2, Hibs' scorers being O'Rourke and Stevenson. Hibs lined up as follows: Allan, Shevlane, Davis, Stanton, Madsen, Blackley, Marinello, Quinn, Cormack, O'Rourke, Stevenson.

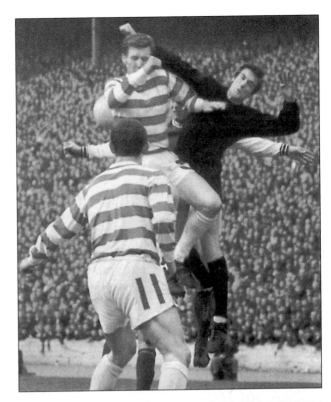

'Keeper Thomson Allan smothers the ball to foil Celts Stevie Chalmers and Bobby Lennox.

Striker Joe McBride was Hibernian's top goalscorer in seasons 1968/69 and 1969/70. Born in Glasgow on 10 June 1938, Joe arrived in Edinburgh on 5 November 1968 from Celtic as a replacement for Colin Stein, at a cost of £15,000. A man of many clubs, including Killie, Wolves, Luton, Partick Thistle, Motherwell, Celtic, Hibs, Dunfermline and Clyde, McBride was a consistent marksman. He retired in 1972, having represented both Scotland and the Scottish League. His son Joe junior later also played for Hibernian, from 1985 to 1988.

Hibernian, 1970/71 season. From left to right, back row: Shevlane, Jones, Brownlie, Black, Marshall, Blair, Stanton, Blackley, Schaedler. Front row: Cropley, Duncan, Hamilton, Graham, McBride, Stevenson.

Magnificent right half Pat Stanton was originally a sweeper under Jock Stein, but moved up into a midfield role upon the big man's departure to Celtic. Born in Edinburgh on 13 September 1944, he was a product of Salvesen Boys' Club and was farmed out to Bonnyrigg Rose. Pat also played for United Crosslands and Edina Hearts before making the breakthrough at Easter Road in 1963. Capped 16 times by Scotland, he made 399 League appearances and scored exactly 50 goals for Hibs. Stanton ended his playing days with Celtic and subsequently managed Cowdenbeath, Dunfermline Athletic and Hibernian. He later became an Edinburgh licensee.

World-class footballer Pat Stanton with the 1970 Scottish Player of the Year award, to add to the League Cup, Summer Cup and Drybrough Cup honours he won while with Hibernian. In 1976 he teamed up with Jock Stein again, reverting back to his sweeper role, and Celtic took the Double. It would not have happened without the skill and calming influence of the veteran 'Quiet Man'.

Jimmy O'Rourke scores Hibs' equalizer in the 1971 Scottish Cup semi-final replay against Rangers at Hampden Park. The Ibrox club ultimately won 2-1, but only thanks to some desperate defending on their part late in the game.

Seven
Turnbull's Tornadoes
(1971-1975)

It's the beginning of a partnership that pushed Hibs to the forefront of British football as one of the cleverest sides in the game – the day in July 1971, when Eddie Turnbull became manager at Easter Road. Witnessing the signing are former Scotland and Hibs goalkeeper Tommy Younger, and Tom Hart, managing director of the club.

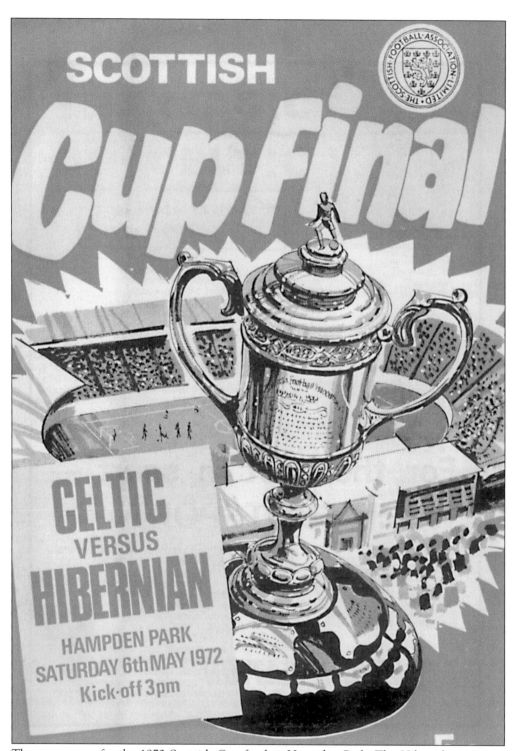

The programme for the 1972 Scottish Cup final at Hampden Park. The Hibees line-up was: Herriot, Brownlie, Schaedler, Stanton, Black, Blackley, Edwards, Hazel, Gordon, O'Rourke and Duncan.

Alan Gordon scores Hibs' equalizer in the 6-1 defeat by Celtic in the 1972 Scottish Cup final. It was the solitary moment of joy on a day best forgotten by Hibernian.

Matchday programme for the 1972/73 Drybrough Cup final, which Hibs won 5-3 after extra time. Celtic levelled the scoreline at 3-3 in ninety minutes after Hibs led 3-0 through an Alan Gordon hat-trick. The Hibs team lined up as follows: Herriot, Brownlie, Schaedler, Stanton, Black, Blackley, Hamilton, Hazel, Gordon, Cropley, Duncan.

Desperate disappointment and anguish is etched on the faces of Erich Schaedler and Pat Stanton as Hibs squander a 3-0 lead in the 1972 Drybrough Cup final. However, two great goals by O'Rourke and Duncan finally won the trophy for Hibs in extra time.

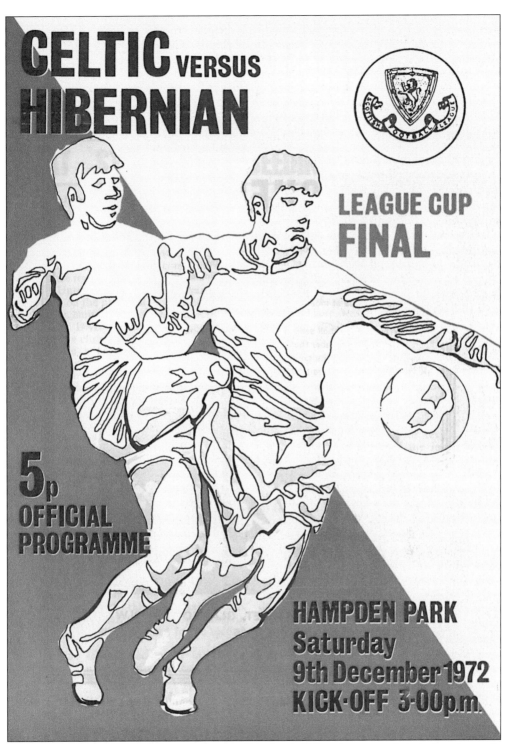

Programme for the 1972/73 Scottish League Cup final. Hibernian secured their first domestic trophy in twenty years with a 2-1 victory over Celtic.

Marvellous captain Pat Stanton sends Hibs on the road to silver success with the opening goal of the 1972/73 Scottish League Cup final at Hampden Park, scored on the hour mark.

Jimmy O'Rourke's flying header puts Hibs 2-0 up after 65 minutes of the 1972/73 League Cup final.

Ticket for the 1972/73 Scottish League Cup final. 71,696 hardy souls congregated on a cold rain-swept Hampden Park to witness Hibernian taking the League Cup on 9 December 1972, with the following team: Herriot, Brownlie, Schaedler, Stanton, Black, Blackley, Edwards, O'Rourke, Gordon, Cropley and Duncan.

SOUTH WEST STAND
Enter at turnstiles
(See Plan on Back)

F

SCOTTISH LEAGUE CUP FINAL
HAMPDEN PARK, GLASGOW
SATURDAY 9th DECEMBER, 1972
KICK-OFF 3.00 p.m.

PRICE £1

Maule,
Secretary

This portion to be retained   Row   Seat No.

The Hibs squad of 1973, pictured with the Drybrough Cup and League Cup. From left to right, back row: Smith, Spalding, McArthur, Bremner, O'Rourke. Middle row: Turnbull, Humphries, Blackley, Murray, Higgins, Brownlie, Black, Fraser, Auld. Front row: Edwards, Schaedler, Munro, Stanton, Gordon, Cropley, Duncan, McNiven.

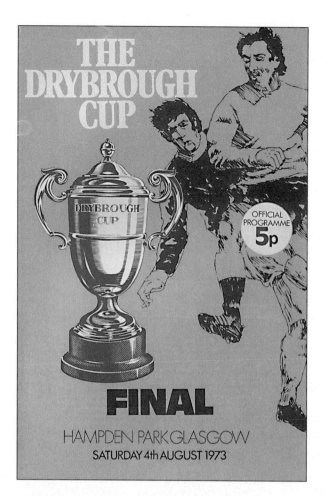

Programme for the 1973/74
Drybrough Cup final against
Celtic. Hibernian won 1-0 after
extra time. The line-up included
youngsters Des Bremner, Tony
Higgins and Iain Munro.

Alan Gordon scores the only goal of the 1973/74 Drybrough Cup final against Celtic at
Hampden Park in the last minute of extra time.

Hibernian's centre forward Alan Gordon challenges St Johnstone's Gordon Smith for a high ball in 1972.

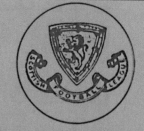

HAMPDEN PARK
SATURDAY 26th OCTOBER 1974
KICK·OFF 3pm

LEAGUE CUP FINAL

CELTIC v HIBERNIAN

Official **5**p
Programme

Matchday programme for the 1974/75 Scottish League Cup final, which Celtic won 6-3. The Hibs team was as follows: McArthur, Brownlie (Smith), Bremner, Stanton, Spalding, Blackley, Edwards, Cropley, Harper, Munro, Duncan (Murray).

Joe Harper nets one third of his hat-trick in the 1974/75 Scottish League Cup final against Celtic.

Marvellous overlapping full-back John Brownlie originally played for Tynecastle Athletic and Edina Hibs and was farmed out to Pumpherston Juniors before making his Hibernian first team debut at Dunfermline in April 1970. Born at Caldercruix on 11 March 1952, he collected 6 full caps for Scotland, before a dreadful double-break injury on 6 January 1973 in a match against East Fife almost ended his career. Brownlie's surging runs down the right flank were a delight to see at Easter Road. He later moved to Newcastle United in exchange for Ralph Callaghan and then joined Middlesbrough in July 1982 for £30,000. Subsequently, he was manager of Cowdenbeath and Meadowbank Thistle, and assistant manager at Clyde.

JOHN BROWNLIE

Tough-tackling Erich Schaedler joined Hibs from Stirling Albion for £7,000 in November 1969. Son of a German father who played for Borussia Munchengladbach, Erich was given his only cap by Willie Ormond for the Scotland against West Germany match in 1974. In November 1977 he moved to Dundee in exchange for Bobby Hutchison, but returned to Easter Road late in 1981. He signed for Dumbarton during the 1985 close season but, tragically, personal problems led to him committing suicide on 24 December 1985, aged thirty-six.

'Sloop' (John B)lackley was born at Westquarter near Falkirk on 12 May 1948. A product of Gairdoch United, he gave Hibernian over a decade of excellent service before joining Newcastle United in October 1977 for £100,000. Capped on 7 occasions by Scotland, Blackley's cool and assured play led to comparisons with Bobby Moore at his best. He subsequently starred at Preston North End and later managed Hamilton Accies, Hibs, Cowdenbeath and Dundee.

Whether on the wing or in midfield, Alex Edwards was a most effective footballer. Always in the thick of the action, 'Micky' was a fiery personality who generally boosted the Easter Road men up front. He first came to prominence at the age of sixteen with Dunfermline, from which club he joined Hibs for £14,000 in October 1971. Edwards was a class act, who had the cunning and balance to deceive the most eagle-eyed defender, but his quick temper saw him sent off six times during his career.

Scottish international winger Arthur Duncan. Like 'Sloop', Duncan played for Gairdoch United, and cost £35,000 from Partick Thistle in January 1970. Born in Falkirk on 5 December 1947, Duncan represented Scotland at all levels: in Schoolboy, Youth, Under-23, Full and Scottish League. Possessing speed and a bewildering body swerve, Arthur was a potential match winner on his own, with the ability to take on defences and accurate finishing. Latterly a left-back, he joined Meadowbank Thistle in 1984.

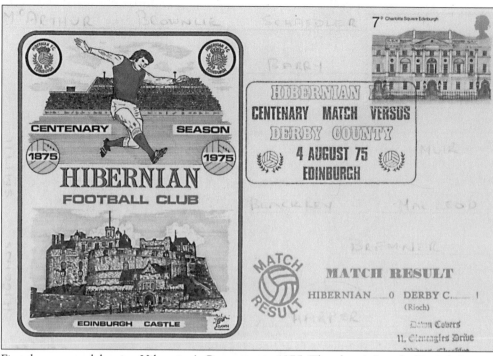

First day cover celebrating Hibernian's Centenary in 1975. They lost 1-0 to the English League Champions Derby County on 4 August 1975. Managed by ex-Hearts man Dave Mackay, Derby's goal was scored by Scotland captain Bruce Rioch.

Hibernian Football Club

A group of Irishmen founded Hibernian in 1875 and, initially, their application to join the S.F.A. was rejected because of their background.

However, the Edinburgh Association welcomed the new club in trying to promote the game and the national body soon relented.

Hibs won their first honour in 1887 by beating Dumbarton 2—1 in the final of the Scottish Cup and established themselves as the best team in the country around the turn of the century.

The Cup returned to Easter Road in 1902 after a win over Celtic and Hibs won the 12-club League by six points in the following season.

Another great side was built in the mid-twenties though they lost the Cup Final in successive years. So, in fact, Hibs' finest period came just after the second world war when the club finished champions three times and runners-up three times in the space of seven years.

Hibs were the first Scottish side to play in the European Champions Cup — by invitation — in 1955 and the first to take part in the Fairs Cup, now called the UEFA Cup. In both cases, Hibs reached the semi-finals.

More recently Hibs have been runners-up twice in the championship and winners of the League Cup in 1972.

HONOURS

Scottish League: Division 1 Champions: 1902-03, 1947-48, 1950-51, 1951-52; Runners-up: 1896-97, 1946-47, 1949-50, 1952-53, 1973-74, 1974-75. Division 2, Champions: 1893-94, 1894-95, 1932-33.
Scottish Cup: Winners: 1887, 1902; Runners-up: 1895-96. 1932-33 1971-72.
Scottish League Cup: Winners: 1972-73; Runners-up: 1950-51, 1968-69.
Drybrough Cup: Winners: 1972-73, 1973-74.
Record Victory: 15-1 v Peebles Rovers, Scottish Cup, 2nd Rd., Feb. 11th, 1961.
Record Defeat: 2-9 v Morton, Division 1, 1918-19.
Most League Points: 54, Division 2, 1932-33.
Most Individual League Goals in Season: 42, Joe Baker, Division 1, 1959-60.
Most Capped Player: Lawrie Reilly, 39, Scotland.
Cover and Handstamp designed by Stuart H. Renshaw (Dawn Cover Productions)
(Designers of the Official Football League Cover Series)

Handstamp of Hibernian FC in 1975. Note that the title of Scottish League Cup runners-up 1974/75 is missing from the honours list.